A Seed Is a]

by Claire Merrill • picture

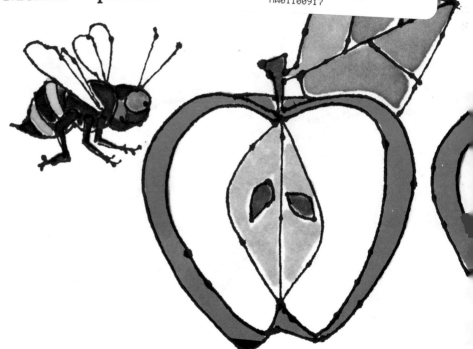

SCHOLASTIC INC.
New York Toronto London Auckland Sydney

ISBN 0-590-43454-3

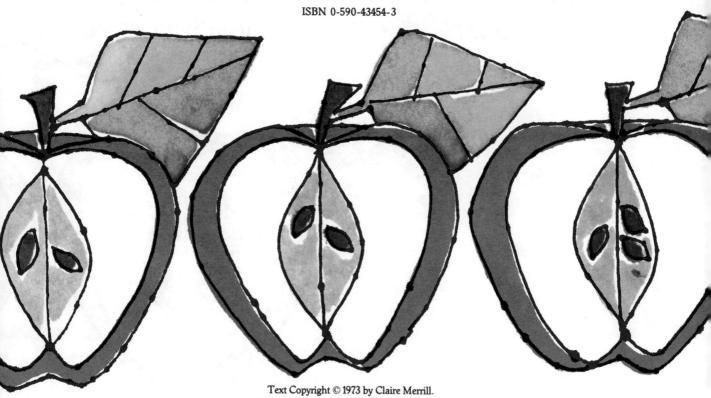

20 19 18 17 16 15 14 13 12   23   89/9012/0

Printed in the U.S.A.

To Mary Birsh with love

You know a lot about seeds.

When you eat an orange,
you see little white seeds inside.

You've seen the seeds of other fruits, too
—apples, pears, melons, grapes.

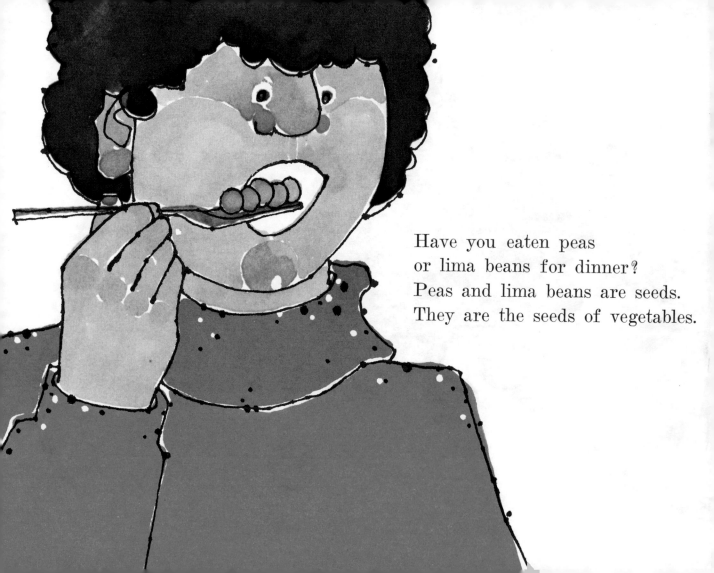

Have you eaten peas
or lima beans for dinner?
Peas and lima beans are seeds.
They are the seeds of vegetables.

Have you ever bought
flower seed packets in the store?
Or fed grass seed to a pet bird?

Have you ever worn maple tree seeds on
your nose?
Or played tea party with the seeds of an oak tree?

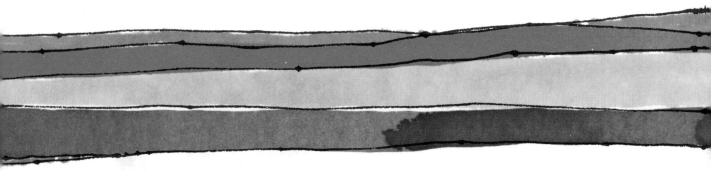

Do you know where all these seeds come from?
All seeds come from plants.

And in every seed there is a promise,
the promise that a new plant will grow.

If you know what kind of plant a seed comes
from, you know what it will grow into.

A bean seed will grow into a bean plant.
An orange seed will grow into an orange tree.
But an orange seed will never grow into a
lemon tree.

How are seeds made? Most seeds begin inside flowers.
Look at the center part of the flower.
This is called the pistil.
At the bottom of the pistil there are tiny egg cells.

Now look at the parts around the pistil.
These are the stamens.
They make a yellow powder called pollen.

A grain of pollen must reach an
egg cell to make a seed.

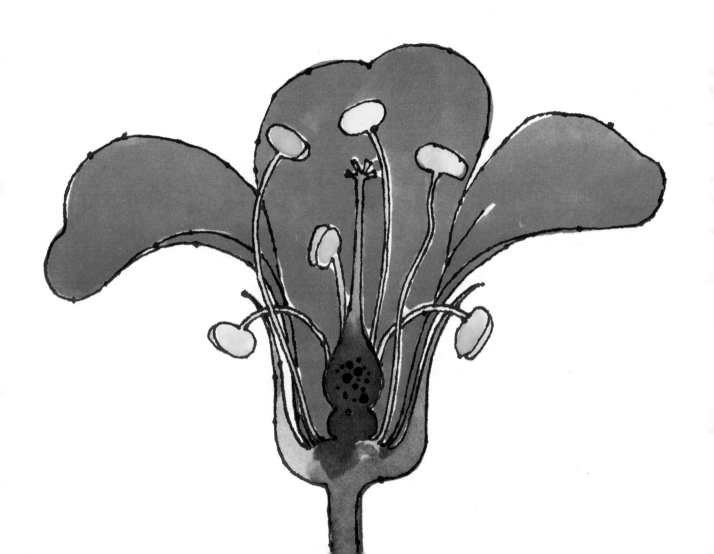

Some flowers use their own pollen to make seeds.
But most flowers use the pollen of other flowers.

Bees and other insects carry pollen from flower
to flower.
Wind blows pollen through the air.

A grain of pollen lands on the pistil of a flower.
The pollen grain grows a long tube down into
the pistil and joins an egg cell.
A seed begins.

Soon the flower starts to die.
Its petals dry and fall.
The flower dies, but inside the pistil
new seeds are growing.

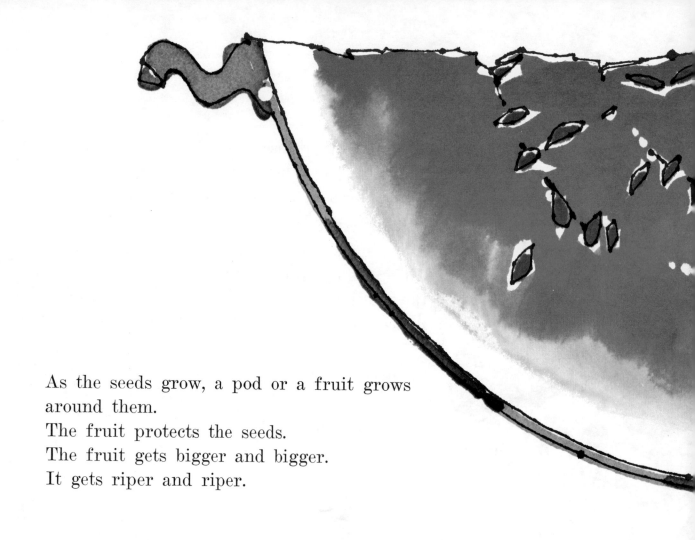

As the seeds grow, a pod or a fruit grows
around them.
The fruit protects the seeds.
The fruit gets bigger and bigger.
It gets riper and riper.

The fruit breaks open.
The seeds are ready to start new plants.

Some seeds fall to the ground right next
to the plant that made them.

Other seeds travel.

The seeds of violets and pansies
shoot into the air.

Milkweed and dandelion seeds
ride silken strands into the wind.

Some seeds have sturdy wings that let
them glide on the wind or float on the water.

Some seeds travel with your help or
even with your dog's.
Their sharp little burrs hook onto clothing
or fur.

Not all of these seeds will grow into plants.
Many things may go wrong.

A seed may not land on good earth.
It may land on a rock, or in your house.
A hungry bird or squirrel may eat it.

But almost every seed starts out with a
chance to grow.
You can find out why.

Soak a lima bean
in water overnight.
In the morning,
let your mother or father
help you cut the seed in half.

Inside you will see
a tiny baby plant.

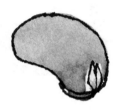

There is a tiny baby plant curled up tight
in every seed.
This tiny plant can grow into a big plant.

And as long as the tiny plant stays alive, there is
a chance that the seed can keep its promise
—even after a very long time.

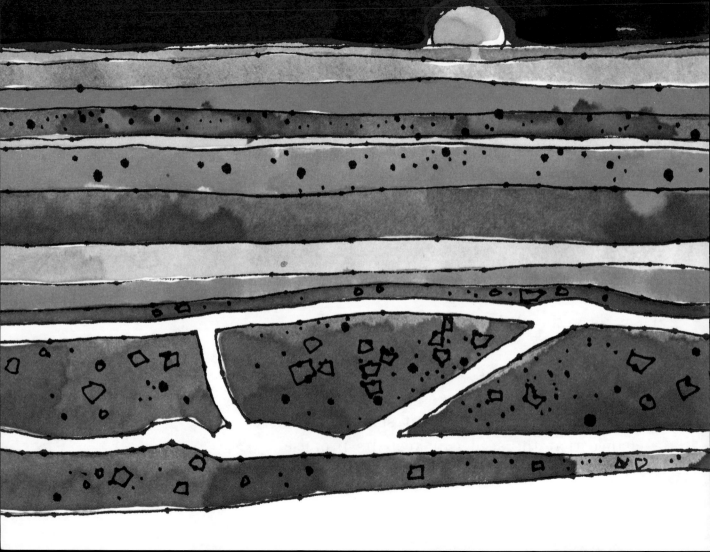

Here is a true story about some seeds that grew
after a *very very* long time.

One day in the cold north country of Canada
a miner was digging in the frozen earth.

Deep down, he found some old animal burrows.
Inside the burrows were some animal bones.
Next to the bones were tiny seeds.

The miner took the bones and seeds.
He showed them to some scientists.

The scientists found out that the bones
were the bones of little animals called lemmings.
The bones were very very old.

Thousands and thousands of years ago, in prehistoric times, the lemmings must have stored the seeds for food.

Everyone wondered, could such old seeds still grow?
Had the earth acted like the freezer in your refrigerator?
Had it kept the seeds from spoiling?

The scientists put the seeds on special wet paper and waited.

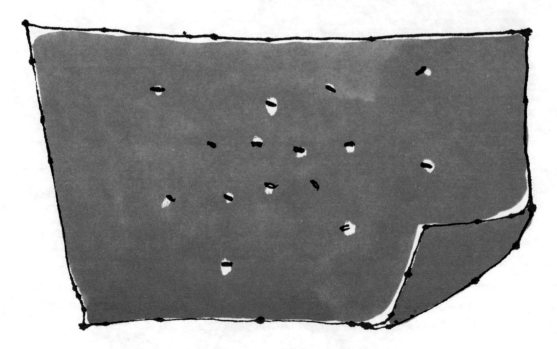

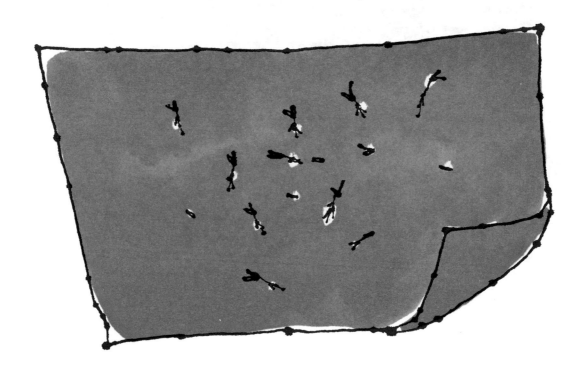

Two days later, this is what they saw.
Some of the seeds had kept their promise.
They had sprouted after thousands and thousands of years.

In time the seeds grew into healthy plants.
The plants grew flowers.
The flowers made new seeds—each with a promise of its own.